CHRIST IS THE HOLY WORD

SCRIPTURE INTERPRETING SCRIPTURE

JOSEPH S. NKOLE

Table of Contents

Joseph S. Nkole

Acknowledgements

Many thanks go to those who have individually or collectively motivated the writing of this book.

I will not forget to appreciate the servant of

God, my mentor, Bishop Dr. Maxwell Musonda, who has been an example and in helping to feed my understanding on the scriptures gracefully.

I thank my brethren for their encouragements concerning the word of God.
May God bless you!

Above all, I give thanks to the almighty God who has privileged me to be in his end time program. His grace and mercy over my life, ministry and family have been quite immeasurable. May His name be praised!

- Joseph S. Nkole

CHRIST IS THE HOLY WORD

Introduction

The body of Christ is in need of understanding of the things that pertain to the kingdom of light. In this book, I choose to express eternal gratitude to God our Father for according me this deeper knowledge of his word. The holy book of the voice of God, as it is has deep treasures that reveal truth. Christ Jesus is our redeemer and Saviour. He has enlightened my mind to explain the scriptures interpreting scripture more and more. If we choose to learn from man, we should say it is not enough to understand the deep things of God. In his own time he chooses to teach us more. For the spirit quickens all things and brings them to light.

I will talk about Jesus Christ as the holy word and the bread of life. We want to look into these two words: Word and Bread. Therefore, enriching the Christian conscience on Jesus, enhancing all it takes and makes to live life serving the Lord today. We have put scripture references to support the words as they are expressed in this book. The scriptures used comparably are from the King James Version (KJV), others are Amplified (AMP) and Holman Standard Christian Bibles (HCSB) and other bible versions.

The Lord God I praise eternally.

THE FATHER, SON AND HOLY SPIRIT

To the holy book my look I hook.
The best book I ever took.
The best tip I keep. On its make I speak.
I lick its love and have no lack.
In its salt, I soothe. Its root I ever sought.
I have its milk I get no mock.
In its holy brook my spirit I soak.

John 8:43 *Why do ye not understand my speech?*
even because ye cannot hear my word. [KJV]

The disciples, other people and Pharisees were new to the doctrine of Jesus. He find out that after he taught them something; in practical times he could not see the meaning of his actions. Later, they asked from him to know the meaning of what he just said. The word of God is strong such that on earth it is compared to a stone. Jesus walked on the water fulfilling his word by demonstrating that through his word he created the water so he walked on his word. The disciples were new to the doctrine of Jesus.

Speech *is a noun [mass noun] the expression of or the ability to express thoughts and feelings by articulate sounds.* [Oxford Dictionary]

To understand the scripture and the mind of Jesus Christ fully, man has to study the word of God. This is also the faculty of uttering articulate sounds or words, as in human beings; the faculty of expressing thoughts by words. The word is spirit. I can as well say that day to day utters speech, and night to night shows knowledge. All the things the Lord God created do speak. As King David the servant of the Lord speaks in Psalms 65.12; the grass sings.

For a man to understand any agreement it means that the way of talk is plainly gotten clearly and can easily be applied for in practice. For language is not enough to say that we know what it is that it being said to our ears when someone is saying something. We do not exactly get an instruction that may clearly has had been explained if we did not get what speech it is in what has be expressed. There is spoken, written and street or common language.

In **Psalms 19:3** *There are no speeches or words, in which their voices are not heard.* [Complete Apostle's Bible]

First we see and know, then read the word even as the voice is heard saying things being read inside our hearts; as we read without opening the mouth. We use the inner or audible voice.

John 6:63 *It is the Spirit who gives life; the flesh is no help at all. The words that I have spoken to you are spirit and life.* [English Standard Version]

Jesus brought the gospel of truth - talking about himself as the truth; he is the messenger as well. The life of the spirit affects the actions.

Jesus said that, "I am the WAY" - the door, gate and the permission to enter heaven - ' I AM' is the name of his father - YAHWEH and he and his Father are one. The will of God is the gate.

The truth – the right to get the stand affirmed, tried and set at peace. The truth leads to goodness as a shepherd.

The life - the way that shows instructions to his people: how to live and act in truth and the only truth which then gives man power to live. Life depends on food in this context the pasture for the sheep of his fold. Jesus is the shepherd and the church is the sheep. According to John 10.1 reading forth.

Men of God are allowed to speak God's hallowed oracles because the spirit lives in them. "But when the Comforter is come, whom I will send unto you from the Father, even the Spirit of truth, which proceedeth from the Father, he shall testify of me:" In the volume of the book, it is written about his children. All that is in the Bible talks about the livehood of his children.

Jesus gives eternal life. No one comes to the Father except through Jesus. He enters our lives and lives in us and with us. He is the gate, the passage and he holds the door keys.

In the very manner, we are on earth and addressed to as somebody's brother, neighbour, friend, nephew, uncle, all these names and not just names but functions for one person like you and I. These are not titles. They are never changed as long as we live. Yet, not confusing and disturbing. We have God the Father, Son and Holy Spirit. They are one. This is found in the book of Isaiah chapter 9.6.

For to us a Child is born, to us a Son is given; and the government shall be upon His shoulder, and His name shall be called Wonderful Counselor, Mighty God, Everlasting Father [of Eternity], Prince of Peace. [Isa. 25:1; 40:9-11; Matt. 28:18; Luke 2:11.] [Amplified Bible]

All these names are proving the the function purpose and unity of the Godhead, the triune God and the trinity. They show what and how the work of God is. This brings us to an understanding of three in a bond and known as the trinity.

Jesus was born as an ordinary child on earth, given as a gift and sacrifice for the sinners and to redemption that he spoke through the mouth of the prophets and fulfilling his written word. Jesus Christ is a surety for a better covenant; his blood speaks better things; a sacrifice for many sins; a ransom for our sins. The price paide for whatever man had lost after falling into sin. The names show the Son of God being Lord in the spiritual state.

The word is spirit therefore it became transformed into flesh. The spirit formed the flesh. At one time Jesus asked his disciples what was greater; the clothes or the body and they answered that the body was greater. Then he asked again which was greater, the body or the soul, they answered that it was the soul. Then he asked. What was greater between the soul and the spirit; as they answered that the spirit was greater. He wanted them to know that they were spirits living in mortal bodies. He came to transform his people from a terrestrial to a celestial body. A celestial body is spiritual. It can pass through a wall. This happened when Jesus of Nazareth was ressurrected: he could pass through walls. He was found in the midst of the disciples. Even if they had the door locked.

When Abraham was visited by the holy Angels;

they came in terrestrial body forms. So they ate food that men eat at Abraham's place. It is written in the book of Hebrews that Abraham by faith entertained Angels without knowledge.

John 10:30 *I and my Father are one.* [King James Version]

The son did what he saw the father doing while he spent time on earth. Whatever he did on earth was also legitimate in heaven. He had the full support of his father. He also said that he would not do anything unless the father agreed with him. He later prayed in gethsemane asking his father if he could allow him to be spared from what he was going to pass through. Seeing it was going to be painful and humiliating. His last words were that the will of the father take lead and not his own will as the son.

Before action, a Christian is supposed to let our father in Heaven know about what their particular intention or plan is. It is good for anyone who has known the purpose of life on earth in Christ Jesus. If this becomes the case then man will not know disappointment. Sudden incidents are never to be part of their lives. More so, the bible has predicted whatsoever events that meets the children of God in their relative lives and the way to live by. When the word gets well known in our minds - it is the making of our thoughts and actions.

John 1:14 *And the Word [or, the Expression of [divine] Logic] became flesh and tabernacled among us, and we beheld His glory, glory as of an only-begotten [or, uniquely-begotten] from [the] Father, full of grace and truth.* [Analytical Literal Translation]

First of all, in the first book in the old testament of the bible. The Father gives authority to create, allows and hallows according to his will. Jesus said, "But that the world may know that I love the Father; and as the Father gave me commandment, even so I do."

The son created all things and all things were made by him and through him. He is the grace and the truth hence the scripture says he is full of grace and truth - for my Father is greater than I. The Father is the authority and Jesus is the power so he expresses truth saying, "and the word which ye hear is not mine, but the Father's which sent me." The Father is spirit and the son is the word of God.

The Holy Spirit is the voice or breath. That says as the Father says and as agreed to be said and done by the Father, Son and Holy Ghost. Jesus said, "When the comforter comes, he shall speak about me."

Therefore any saint that walks in truth and does the will of God and is called by the name of God has the right to be called a son of God. He has obtained authority and power and self-will. Jesus once told the disciples that the servant does not know what his master is doing but a friend. When they had all known his will; he started calling them friends.

The right every human being has - is to choose whatsoever they wish in life while on earth. Abraham was God's friend so he was able to know God's plan as in the case when God planned to destroy Sodom. He informed Abraham about it.

Witnesses

I John 5:7 *For there are three that bear record in heaven, the Father, the Word, and the Holy Ghost: and these three are one. 8 And there are three that bear witness in earth, the spirit, and the water, and the blood: and these three agree in one.* [KJV]

Heaven | Earth

The Father | The Spirit
The Word | The Water
The Holy Ghost | The Blood

The covenant keeping witnesses. The will of

God says that the Father is who is in Spirit or the Holy Spirit, is the highest authority. He is Judge of judges; King of Kings and God of God. It is written in scripture, "Hear, O Israel; The Lord our God is one Lord:" Deutronomy 17.6

The Father is in the son and the son in the Father - Headship. When you see the son, you have seen the Father and when you see the Father, you have seen the Son - Lordship. The Father and Son are one, in the son himself - sonship.

The son has the fullness of the Godhead bodily in him. He is the word of God who is the holy water; he is transparent; honest, true - allows men to pass through him to the Father and be purged clean through his righteousness in glory; no one goes to the Father except through him. By his name we are saved and safe.

The Father in the Holy Spirit, the Holy Spirit in the Father. The Father is the Spirit, the Spirit is the Father.

The Holy Spirit on earth and Holy Ghost in heaven; he is judge of his people. He redeems permanently from sin. Jesus said in the book of John, "Nevertheless I tell you the truth; It is expedient for you that I go away: for if I go not away, the Comforter will not come unto you; but if I depart, I will send him unto you."

The Father is spirit therefore they that worship him should worship him in truth and in spirit. The Father, Son and Holy Ghost are one – Kingship.

The blood smeared on the door posts in Egypt by the Israelites was provided for as a Passover from darkness, unfruitfulness, sin, sickness and death. This is the blood of a blameless Lamb of God. This statute was given to Israelites by Moses. The blood speaks, fights, sets free, works on behalf his children - as a lawyer. The blood has specific works that could be accessed by redeemed men. It is up to man to make a petition according to the need that should be address by the blood. It is the blood that bought men from darkness to light. It can be used as a currency (form of exchange) to pay for debts of those in question or found with such a request towards Yahweh the Lord. Leviticus 5.1

In a court of law, if the men's testimonies contradicted one another on important points, their witness was invalidated. The three give witness one for the other. There evidence is the same in all-three. Apostle Paul teaches in the book of 2 Corithians 13.1 that when two or three people speak about the same matter in unison, there is establishment follow-through. Whatever is spoken in oath, binds. It stands as men have sweared. This is the making of a covenant. Usually when covenants are made like a marriage; two people marry and the man who stands there to witness and see it bonded. The ancient form of attestation is found in this book, Ruth 4.1-11.

When God the Father decided to create man, he made a covenant with the Son and Holy Spirit. He said, "Let us." He made sure that they agreed on the vision.

This is why when he makes something, no other person and figure that was not there when he was actually making it should put asunder to what he has made. When the devil made Adam lose the way. He was not in the covenant of creating man, so God put back together what he had made good get restored. God as a covenant keeper.

All is spiritual as it pertains to the invisible and only wise God. He is invisible in the physical and spiritual world. No one has ever seen him except his son, Jesus. Moses wanted to to see his face at mount Sinai. he was told that if he saw the face of Yahweh, he would die.

BAPTISM

Let us talk about the three witnesses on earth which is also the reality and truth of a Christian life.

John 4.24 *God is a Spirit: and they that worship him must worship in spirit and truth.* [American Standard Version]

1John 5:6 *This is he who came by water and by blood, Jesus Christ; not by water only but by water and by blood.* [1965 Bible in Basic English]

John 3:5 *Jesus answered, Verily, verily, I say unto*

thee, Except a man be born of water and of the Spirit, he cannot enter into the kingdom of God. [Ezek. 36:25-27.] [Amplified Bible]

John 19:34 *But one of the soldiers with a spear opened his side: and immediately there came out blood and water.* [1899 Douay-Rheims Bible]

A man who is in need of freedom may agree with what the word says and the life of what the holy word stands for. The Bible says that where the spirit of God is, there is liberty. The Holy word comes as a law in the first place which shows men there standing with the one who created them. The spoken word used to agree or believe - becomes the statement used as evidence of right standing with the Lord.

The Blood is for total deliverance and water for cleansing.

The blood is a lawyer for all men that seek to be liberated. The blood speaks fights, ransoms and negotiates in cases where someone needs to settle matters. The blood is the reading of the record of a man who is in question according to the statute of the word. It is used to buy freedom of men. Because that the son of God in whom there was found no sin took all sin and became a sinner that those that would seek redemption may through him and by him find it. It fights any wars and battles that a man who has attained salvation may face along his journey. Since the day of John the Baptist, men ought to fight for freedom. When The Baptist was beheaded, the Lord declared war.

This is done using the holy word as an assurance and insurance. They affirm what and where they stand. The word is used for testimony both spoken and written in the books of the law and life.

There is spiritual Baptist – that consolidates all things accomplished by Jesus on earth. John said that one who was to come after him baptized in the Holy Ghost and fire. So, we could say the baptism of fire seals all that we need to attain for his glory. Jesus ushers in men, the work of the Holy Ghost.

Joseph S. Nkole

The blood consecrates and sanctifies us – making us ready for the great commission.

Blood Baptism

R eading Romans 10.9 Man believes in his heart and confesses with his lips that Christ is Lord. And a great conversion takes place making what is impossible with man possible only with God almighty from being a Sinner to a Saint.

Exodus 12.7 And they shall take of the blood, and strike it on the two side posts and on the upper door post of the houses, wherein they shall eat it.

8 And they shall eat the flesh in that night, roast with fire, and unleavened bread; and with bitter herbs they shall eat it.

9 Eat not of it raw, nor sodden at all with water, but roast with fire; his head with his legs, and with the purtenance thereof.

10 And ye shall let nothing of it remain until the morning; and that which remaineth of it until the morning ye shall burn with fire.

11 And thus shall ye eat it; with your loins girded, your shoes on your feet, and your staff in your hand; and ye shall eat it in haste: it is the LORD's *Passover.*

12 For I will pass through the land of Egypt this night, and will smite all the firstborn in the land of Egypt, both man and beast; and against all the gods of Egypt I will execute judgment: I am the LORD.

13 And the blood shall be to you for a token upon the houses where ye are: and when I see the blood, I will pass over you, and the plague shall not be upon you to destroy you, when I smite the land of Egypt.

14 And this day shall be unto you for a memorial; and ye shall keep it a feast to the LORD throughout your generations; ye shall keep it a feast by an ordinance forever. [KJV]

In all this is the redemption of God's children spiritually. When the children of Israel put blood of the lamb on the door posts is as man confesses through his lips and asks Christ to wash his soul with the blood of the lamb, his mouth is eternally protected from destruction by disease and when the Angel of death who is the Lord Jesus, came to smite the land of Egypt of its first born sons, passed over there houses: They were protected from the power of death.

First born children were highly regarded and entitled to carry the name of the family to the next generation. They inherited Kingship. So it is for a new born again Christian. An order is supposed to be kept in a soldier's memory. 2 Timothy 2:4.

He prays the sinner's prayer and blood seals on his lips protecting anything corrupt to enter his system - he has eternal life. This is an incorruptible life. A life free from malice, vice and evil device power. Man is restored to be a son of God again. Instead of dying he sleeps to wait for the Lord's Day. Jesus Christ second coming to get his own to heaven. Just like the first fruit. The tenth of every harvest of a property; life of man; time and the realisation of income has to be given unto God. This is called Tithe. You may read in the book of Malachi 3.9-10.

This is the greatest work of salvation. That it seperates man from sin. Without salvation men suffer in the slavery of sin.

Water Baptism

It is done in a body of water, river and swimming pool. When a man is immersed in the water during baptism - he simply dies with Christ; and as he comes out of the water - resurrects with him. He is resurrected, a new born person in the spirit. Mark 1.8 *I indeed have baptized you with water...* John the Baptist was baptizing the people with water. This is done for repentance of sins. It is a public demonstration that a man has turn away from sin. The old is gone behold the new has come. It is the purging away of sins. A man is therefore endowed with authority.

Water is used for washing the soul clean. The water is the word of God in Ephesians 5:26. In John 15.3 Jesus Christ says that his disciples are clean because of the word that he spoke to them. We know after this that water is for cleaning. It sustains life. The earth contains 70 percent of water so as the human body. After justification by accepting Christ in our hearts, redemption comes when the soul has been redeemed from sin by the blood of Jesus Christ which he shed on the cross of Calvary, in repentance man passes through cleansing by the water.

Also Luke 3.16

Water supports life. In the making of the bread – it is used to put the flour and other ingredients together. So does the word of God – it brings the people back to their God. It keeps them in his presence, it is a guide and guard; it is key for all the instructions from the Lord.

Many things were created from the water. It constitutes in many things made.

.

Spiritual baptism

It was the life of Christ on earth which is one with how John the Baptist was born and ministered to the Lord God. It is the baptism that gives a Christian power.

About John it is written in Luke chapter 1:80 And the child grew, and waxed strong in spirit, and was in the deserts till the day of his showing unto Israel.

About Jesus, it is written in Luke chapter 2:40 And the child grew, and waxed strong in spirit, filled with wisdom: and the grace of God was upon him. Mark 1.8 … Jesus would baptize you with the Holy Ghost.

Luke 3:16 John answered, saying unto them all, I indeed baptize you with water; but one mightier than I cometh, the latchet of whose shoes I am not worthy to unloose: he shall baptize you with the Holy Ghost and with fire:

John explained that the shoes that mean his peace; that Jesus was to be putting on; no man could destroy. He should meaning he just have to baptise you with the Holy Ghost and with fire. As his children are restored back to him. We need to have an eternal protection and provision always while we are on earth where the enemy also is roaming to and fro, looking for whom he may devour.

But the Holy Spirit does this -

17 Whose fan is in his hand, and he will throughly purge his floor, and will gather the wheat into his garner; but the chaff he will burn with fire unquenchable.

He is capable of getting his people together and ordaining them as worthy of his love using his unquencheable fire. John the Baptist was preparing the way of the Lord Jesus Christ who physically was born after John. Yet spiritually he was there before John. Jesus Christ justifies, cleanses, sanctifies a believer and circumcises the mind after purification unto holiness.

He who dwells in the secret place of the most high shall abide in the shadow of the almighty. It is a secret to be a Christian because it is a mystery, seeing how it happens. It is unknown to common or natural senses. The word of the Lord in the bible is written in black as a shadow of a man is black; we could say it's dark as well.

I believe that, a man who studies the word with faith as shown in Hebrews 4:2; is always abiding in great comfort. It is of great joy to the Lord to see his children watch over his word and act according to his word.

*No understanding; no access to
knowledge and wisdom.*

It happened on the day of Pentecost, when the saints received the gift of the spirit after understanding their purpose and calling. I had a chance to leave my country and travelled to another. There I learnt the power of language that whenever we spoke in our own language in a public place - the natives of that country would wonder if we hardly knew any bit of their language.

Having no knowledge about a particular language is a barrier for communication. It is impossible to have a prosperous relationship in that way. It has to be acquired by way of learning the skill by and by. The saints who have received the gift of the spirit have also received faith language which is one in the body of Christ; the church.

A child is first intrigued by sound and then he is taught language, after which he gets understand of the names of things; how he is going to live in life and right and wrong. Finally, his life in society becomes easy to live by.

The Lord made sure to give his saints a language that no man could understand. Language is for communication but also could be used for offense against enemies and defense; protection from destruction.

Paul spoke about tongues saying that we speak in groans that no man can utter. We build ourselves when we pray in this heavenly language. The benefits of speaking in holy tongues are immeasurable.

We see how the disciples waited to be baptized and get endowed with power of fire from the Lord god Yahweh in the book of Luke 2.

Acts 2.1 *And when the day of Pentecost was fully come, they were all with one accord in one place.*

2. And suddenly there came a sound from heaven as of a rushing mighty wind, and it filled all the house where they were sitting.

3. And there appeared unto them cloven tongues as of fire, and it sat upon each of them.

4. And they were all filled with the Holy Ghost and began to speak in other tongues, as the Spirit gave them utterance.

For a man to be led by the Spirit and walk in the

spirit; he needs to receive the Holy Spirit and speak in tongues as of fire. A man who has emptied their conscience that was formerly filled up with sinful information. In order to have it filled it in with the holy word. The Holy Spirit will operate well in a heart that has no grudge and other sins that man has not forgiven others or himself .

Christ a seed yet food to feed on
A reed in his holy brook,
He breaks not for he leads so we heed to
A need for every creed.

LIFE

Life depends and feeds on knowledge - the pasture of the sheep of Jesus Christ. The pasture is the deisre of his sheep. The wisdom for his church. I want to take leaf from the very first book of the holy book. So that every word is revealed in its entire use to shade more light on what the word of God teaches us. And not to take the bible as a mere book but one that contains life. In the book of -

Genesis 1:

1. In the beginning God created the heaven and the earth.

2. And the earth was without form, and void;

and darkness was upon the face of the deep. And the Spirit of God moved upon the face of the waters.

3. And God said, Let there be light: and there was light.

Rust, lust, dust, in the most of life
We must cast out and avoid,
Lest, for you; about you and of you
it's a haste to the void.

In verse 2 of Genesis chapter 1, in the heart of a sinner is a void, darkness. So light comes in them to enlighten, make alive what was dead. This is accomplished by way of acceptance of the truth which is also light.

In - *preposition expressing the situation of something that is or appears to be enclosed or surrounded by something else; expressing a value as a proportion of (a whole); expressing inclusion or involvement; to be or keep in with, to be close or near.* [Oxford dictionary]

In *denotes present, surrounded by limits; as in a house; in a fort; in a city. It denotes a state of being mixed, as sugar in tea; or combined, as carbonic acid in coal, or latent heat in air.* [Webster Bible Dictionary 1828]

John 1.4 *IN him was life; and the life was the light of men.* [KJV]

In God is life everlasting (immortal) and when he speaks he speaks life. The life of God is as pure as light and holy. I will further look into the use of light. Jesus Christ yoke is ease and his burden is light. It has less weight. It does not require one to use fleshly efforts which lead people to dire consequences.

In the Lord God were all things before creation. With him and all things were made for him.

Psalms 119:140 *Thy word is very pure: therefore thy servant loveth it.* [1833 Webster Bible]

Proverbs 30:5 *Every Word of God is refined, He is a shield to those who seek refuge in Him.* [Literal Translation of the Holy Bible]

Psalms 18:30 *As for God, his way is perfect. The word of LORD is tried. He is a shield to all those who take refuge in him.* [A Conservative Version]

God- *His way is perfect; the word of the LORD is pure. He is a shield to all who take refuge in Him.* [HSCB]

As for God, His way is perfect! The word of the Lord is tested and tried; He is a shield to all those who take refuge and put their trust in Him. [AMP]

Knowing about the word is like belief and living it - is like breathe and it is spiritual. This is the reality of the life in Christianity. The work of God is believing in him.

John 10.10 *... I am come that they might have life, and that they might have it more abundantly.* [Kings James Version]

I AM signifying the name of God, Jehovah, and El. [Exodus 3.13 *And Moses said unto God, Behold, when I come unto the children of Israel, and shall say unto them, The God of your fathers hath sent me unto you; and they shall say to me, What is his name? what shall I say unto them? 14 And God said unto Moses, I AM that I AM: and he said, Thus shalt thou say unto the children of Israel, I am hath sent me unto you.]* [KJV]

Come Jesus Christ calling the father from heaven

That his reason for coming to the earth for dead, sinful people

They the sinners, world

Might - *modal verb [3rd singular. present might) past of May, used especially in reported speech, to express possibility or permission,* [Oxford dictionary], because man has self-will, so he chooses to get permission to get life or death].

Have life everlasting, eternal

And that for a reason; permission; right

They his people, church, Christians,

Might have receive, obtain, attain **it** knowledge, authority, power, faith

More abundantly continuously, everlasting, in full measure; plenty; and provision.

2 Chronicles 14:7 The Lord uses the word **if**, v.t. *It is used as the sign of a condition, or it introduces a conditional sentence. It is a verb, without a specified nominative.*

A man is given permission only after asking for that which he requires. We enter in the holy of holies through Christ Jesus, the door and shepherd.

John 16:24 *Hitherto have ye asked nothing in my name: ask, and ye shall receive, that your joy may be full.*

In John chapter 10 *he says that they **might*** and in John 16 he says **ask** so this means we have a choice to get life or death.

Though it is freely given, the condition is to agree to ask to get life and step in eternity. Christ Jesus asked from the Father for us and we have received the gift of life in full. Yet, we have self-will so we choose between life and death.

He also says '**If**' my people shall turn away from their wicked ways. The condition is If and it means that only when one decides to get life, there is life at their disposal. When understanding is full enough it is then called knowledge. If we have the right standing; we hereby are strengthened up to mighty. We can apply what we have in our conscience. After being worked out in the mind; it can then be embedded in our conscious then in the conscience.

He is on the run meaning always running and or keeps running. It is like a moving train that one gets on while it is running. Here, we are not talking about where the train is from but that it's ever moving in motion.

THE - *This adjective is used as a definitive, that is, before nouns which are specific or understood; or it is used to limit their signification to a specific thing or things, or to describe them;*

BEGINNING - noun, *the point in time or space at which something begins.*

As a verb (present participle) - *participles In grammar, a participle is a form of a verb that can be used in compound tenses of the verb. There are two participles in English: the past participle, which usually ends in `-ed', and the present participle, which ends in `-ing'.*

It is continuous, alive, process that happens on and on now. Always happening, active, whenever, a Sinner converts to a Saint. In the bible it states that, in the very heart of the Sinner light comes in and the darkness, sin, ignorance cannot comprehend it. When a Sinner believes in his heart and confesses with his mouth.

2 Corinthians 5:17 *Therefore, if anyone is in Christ, he is a new creation; the old has passed away, behold, the new has come.* [Common Edition, New Testament - CENT]

This transfiguration is that the new man is ever new. The taking of what was corrupt and regeneration to something new that is incorrupt.

Galatians 6:15 *For in Christ Jesus neither circumcision nor uncircumcision means anything, but a new creation.* [English Majority Text Version]

Romans 10.8 *What does it say, then? The word is very near to you; it is in your mouth and in your heart, that is, the word of faith, the faith which we preach,*

9 that if you declare with your mouth that Jesus is Lord, and if you believe with your heart that God

raised him from the dead, then you will be saved.
[New Jerusalem Bible]

Let us look again at what was in the beginning of creation.

> 1. *In the beginning God created the heaven and the earth.* – [KJV]

1. ***IN THE** beginning **God** (prepared, formed, fashioned, and) created the heavens and the earth.* [Heb. 11:3.] – [AMP]

Creation of heaven and earth was well thought of by Yahweh. He had the right picture of what he wanted to see made manifest. Heaven is in the spiritual realm and the living that are there;have celestial bodies and earth in the physical or material, which are called terrestrial bodies [1Cor. 15.40]. About heaven, I would say that it is a celestial form while earth is terrestrial. The spiritual realm is a source of many unimaginable created things we see and cannot see, touch and cannot touch, reach and cannot reach.

For as much as we are Christians we are to search and seek the face of Yahweh and pray that it be well with us. In Job 12 and Colossians 2 the bible reveals it by announcing the end of lack or the deliverance of man from trouble - for he is actually born into bondage.

This bondage and slavery to sin came when the first Adam sinned and fell from grace. And redemption is promised when the second Adam who is Jesus Christ of Nazareth came to die for all sinners and rose up or resurrected from the dead. Men are, therefore, given all the privileges to attain life everlasting by choice. Henceforth, the life everlasting was freely given. No matter the years served in the Lord Yahweh on earth, without asking we could be as good as having nothing at all. Only thieves get things without asking who the owner is and without regards to whom they belong. It is a legal Christian right to ask and receive according to the will of the Lord.

Jesus in the book of Luke teaches his disciples to plan before engaging in any worthy project. He says that no man builds a mansion without counting the cost of the whole project. It is wise to strategically plan for all things before starting. [Luke 14.28]

The Lord God has always so loved his creation and after the fall from grace. He made a plan to redeem all through Jesus Christ of Nazareth. In his gospel which is simple. This means that when you hear, you follow through. If not, it is hard to see the holy will of liberty manifest in our personal lives.

This reminds us that when Daniel prayed he opened the window in the east: the source of light on earth and in the spiritual sense – which is to say that he looked to the all mighty Yahweh; the father of lights. When our sight is fixed to light: we are able to see well and lead a peaceful life. Greater light is what we need to spend eternal life on earth and after death and or rapture: in heaven then.

In a common language light is called energy. Energy is found in many forms. And we may know that energy is needed by all living biological things. Including non-living matter. Energy is used in machines to move them and manufacture other products.

THE DEEP

It is the glory of God to conceal the matter but the honour of Kings (Christians) to search it out. As sons and daughters we need to get deep in reading, studying and asking about it. We can look at Samuel and Elisha to know that these men lived at a distance from the people. They spent enough time to seek Yahweh's face. They dug deeper in the knowledge of him. Evidently, they had profound counsel towards the kings of Israel at that time.

As written in the book of Genesis 1 -

Genesis 1.2 *And the earth was without form, void; and darkness was upon the face of the deep.*

Deep means *remote from comprehension, far*

from the outer part; secreted, opposed to shallow; as deep water; whatever is hard to comprehend needs concentration to find answers concern it. [Webster 1828 Dictionary]

When challenges come, they come before our face. God unveils whatever is hidden in men's lives. In other words the scripture says there is no secret under the sun.

A void is a useless, dark, stagnation, hindrance and an unprofitable place before man. It is a hopeless situation; a stumbling block; despair; a moment of indecision and an ungodly spot in one's life. It is a thing that makes men to murmur; make faults; delay; procrastinate.

When things that represent difficult are recognized, studied and understood they become useful after creation because transformation is obvious. After creation there is obviously a good report.

The earth was without form - it had no function, stagnant. It was not fashion for good works yet. It had no life.

The earth was void - It had no meaning, impotent, stunted, barren and useless. It was not suitable for spending life and had no life there.

The earth had darkness - an out of bounds place. A place were no activity is taking place and no man can do his works from. When faced with such a situation, we should get over the matter and speak what we desire and expect to see come out of what it is that is before our face. In the book of Acts 13.11 Saul who was called Paul filled with the holy Ghost cursed the sorcerer Elymas and immediately a mist and darkness covered his eyes and turned blind.

The face of the deep is a matter is the face of the waters is the voice in verse two of Genesis chapter one. It could be the voice of men or the voice of God. The voice speaks about whatever is written and programmed about a man or situation. Yet, in this situation Jehovah spoke, "let there be light." He gave charge to the void for creation's sake.

-ation suffix (*forming nouns*) denoting *an action or an instance of it.* [Oxford dictionary]

In the face, of what we do not know about or in the waters. We have the holy word to use as a tool to create. In the face means when we are confronted by a challenge. We need knowledge to choose what is right to produce. For a man to use right words - he has to get knowledge of Jesus Christ: the mind of Jesus. Jesus created all things, so we can create what we desire through prayer. In prayer, we can ask from Yahweh or for some other things – we can declare believing that the power of Yahweh that was in Jesus and in us is able to make our desire manifest now. Job talks about the shadow of death – a place unknown; a challenge; a trial and or a hard time. He says that Yahweh discovers – he creates.

Job 12:22 *He discovereth deep things out of darkness, and bringeth out to light the shadow of death.* [King James Version]

We need light which is the revelation of knowledge to be able to speak life into a situation. Man was made in Yahweh's image so he creates as well. Men used to imagine about so many things since time immemorial which have now been made in the 21st century. Things that used to be far from the natural world have come to be possible.

Proverbs 18:4 *The words of a man's mouth are deep waters; the fountain of wisdom is a bubbling brook.* [English Standard Version]

Wisdom instructs things to work
as it is applied for.

Genesis 1:2. *And the earth was without form, and void; and darkness was upon the face of the deep.* [King James Version]

2. *The earth was without form and an empty waste, and darkness was upon the face of the very great deep. The Spirit of God was moving (hovering, brooding) over the face of the waters.* – [Amplified Bible]

This scripture emphasizes on the word depth of knowledge of God. The understanding is that profound creations are accomplished by every word that man speaks. In the book of James we read about the power of the tongue. The tongue works many things. An oath or the covenant has power that binds two parties and can never be broken.

What we see verse **2** of Genesis chapter **1**, the word <u>deep</u> *is a place where great treasures are stored, forgotten state or far place,*

The earth was without form – it signifies something that that does not have meaning or a thing that we see for the first time. The deep is a mystery. It is work that requires more effort, focus, skill and knowledge to find it out. It is a daily application of consistent work that adds up to allow us to grow to the full staure of Christ. When we do little bits of work towards a goal, gradually we can build the needed power that we need for any given task.

Ecclesiastes 7:24 *Whatever wisdom may be, it is out of reach. It is deep, very deep. Who can find out what it is?* [God's Word Bible]

Now this is Solomon's and David's expression in Psalms saying:

Psalms 92:5 *How have Your works been magnified, O Lord! Your thoughts are very deep.* [Complete Apostle's Bible]

Psalms 95:4 *In his hand are the depths of the earth, and the mountain peaks belong to him.* [New International Version]

Daniel 2:22 *He opens up the depths, tells secrets, sees in the dark--light spills out of him!* [Message Bible]

He is the light and his light puts all things in revelation. So his sons are able to see those things are in the dark. They can dissolve doubt and interpret proverbs.

Psalms 42:7 *Deep calleth unto deep...* [Kings James Version]

A deep thing is one that is unknown or unfounded. God knows whatever is enclosed. Night is like day to the Lord. A certain man decided to build a house and made sure he was focused to bring into place all that is involved to have his establishments accomplished. First, he was to dig deep down, to keep the purpose and reason of the building pillar; the foundation strong. Or else it may fall down. Of course there is going to be lots of material to be used to build, if the building was to be collapsed by an earthquake and cracks caused by a ground shake. That includes money to buy the materials as well.

In other bible versions they use the word expanse. A firmament is a concrete state that holds the sky in position; th sky is the water that God parted saying that the other water will be up and the other down. So the water that is up is held by the firmament. Without the firmament even the building that men build would not hold against strong winds.

Genesis 1:7 And God made the firmament, and divided the waters which were under the firmament from the waters which were above the firmament: and it was so. [KJV]

A strong foundation resists corruption.

Genesis 1.8 And God called the firmament Heavens (a). [AMP]

The heavens are strong and spiritual. The physical eyes cannot see the heavens. The spiritual affects the physical world.

Genesis 1.9. Then God said, "Let the waters below the heavens be gathered into one place, and let the dry land appear"; and it was so. [New American Standard Bible]

The foundation of every building is important as its longevity depends on it. They hold the whole structure together in one accord and order. The deeper the word sinks in the hearts of his people the stronger the foundation. The word is a system that is on holy direction and organization. A man only reads, the rest is the work of the Lord. He builds on a strong foundation; a rock. He helps us know, understand and follow his instructions to prosper in all our ways and succeed.

The foundations of the earth are invisible to the physical eyes. Just like Christians must have a foundation of their faith made strong by following in on the steps of those that lived such a sacred life before them. These are men who kept the testimony of holiness. The holy word encourages me when it says that Prophet Elijah was a man with passions like us but he prayed for the rain to cease and it did so. He again prayed for the rain to start raining again and it did. The other thing I learn in that scripture is that, Elijah prayed seven times. The servant or in this context the arm bearer; he had was sent to check if there was a sign that the rain would start, the first time he prayed. Now I recognize that the servant did not know well the ways of the Lord. He was still learning. Now, during the seventh time the servant said that he could only see a small cloud, the size of a man fist. And that was what Elijah needed for confirmation that the labour of the prayers he made was answered already. The process time did not matter to Elijah but the sign. He did not mind how long he was going to pray on the matter; all he knew is that Yahweh answers at his will. He knew that diligence in prayer is what is important. A fervent prayer avails much. The moment is he was told about the sign; he stopped praying and began preparing to run and hide under a shelter as there was coming a great down pour after a long time of drought.

Ephesians 2:20 You are like a building with the apostles and prophets as the foundation and with Christ as the most important stone. [Contemporary English Version]

The word deep means that a man is devoted

to doing what they believe. They are skilled in what they have learnt and have decided to keep so. It is a life of profound meaning. It is a life that has a good-standing with the truth. This is not one situation where man talks and walks accordingly only once but a lifelong work.

In the deep can also be said as in a state when we are so knowledgeable and when we are in despair – in the unknown state. A state when a man has no idea about what to do. Henceforth, when we face what we do not understand – we are required to find out more about, around, over it to get to a state of revelation. All things start small - from a word, idea and a seed. For us to build a house – it all starts with one brick or stone. The void can be said that it's also a dark place or any challenge that needs understanding acquisition from the holy word.

Luke 6:48 *He is like a man that built a house; and he dug and went deep, and laid the foundations on a rock: and when a flood occurred, the flood rushed upon that house, and could not move it, for its foundation rested on a rock.* [James Murdock New Testament Bible]

Proverbs 24.2 *For their heart studieth destruction, and their lips talk of mischief.*

3 Through wisdom is an house builded; and by understanding it is established:

4 And by knowledge shall the chambers be filled with all precious and pleasant riches. [KJV]

Whatever the heart studies; it makes whatever it does based on the information it has. For a Christian to stand strong in all seasons, they have to guard the heart. Whatever is in the heart has to be brought out with discretion. The only way to guard the heart is by the holy word. It is the holy word that makes one know how to live by. The heart is a place where wisdom is stored. Here the heart is the spirit of man. The heart is the seat of the Holy Spirit.

If it were that a man was living in wrong; in deceit, it shows that he has had been studying that life way or method hence living up to it. The scripture says you shall know them by their fruits. Our lips would start to speak what we see and is then kept in the heart. And out of the heart then the issues which could either be good or bad. It is in the self-will of man to decide to do according to particular wishes.

Psalms 36.4 *He plans wickedness upon his bed; He sets himself on a path that is not good; He does not despise evil.* [NASB]

Also Genesis 2:21, Genesis 8:2, Genesis 15:12, Genesis 7:11.

THE HOLY WORD

Read the word to get gird, guide and guard.

The Word and the Spirit

Genesis chapter 1.3, God said - Jehovah God + Said (Gen.1.1),

God with the **Word**; the word **Said** - *past tense and past participle of say.*

Say - Adjective - *used in legal language or humorously to refer to someone or something already mentioned or named, made, created. It is something which has form, substance, weight, matter, life in itself.*

Word means *signal; order; command, declaration; purpose expressed.* [Webster 1828 dictionary]

The church which is the body of Christ is built on his word. His people are kept alive by the holy word foundation. The word is spirit and the life, the breathe of the church.

Any word that is spoken has to be supported by the Holy Spirit to be made manifest. The foundation of the worlds was made in the same manner.

And in John 1.1 *In the beginning was the Word, and the Word was with God, and the Word was God.*

2 The same (Word) was in the beginning with God.

3 All things were made by him; and without him was not anything made that was made. [King James Version]

The word that was in Yahweh made all things in heaven and on earth. Later, in the chapter below we learn that the word is Jesus of Nazareth.

Rev 19. 13 *He was wearing a robe that had been soaked in blood, and the name by which he is called is, "THE WORD OF GOD."* [Complete Jewish Bible]

13. *... and the title by which He is called is The Word of God.* [AMP]

Psalms 103:20 *Bless the LORD, O you his angels, you mighty ones who do his word, obeying the voice of his word!* [ESV]

When we read the word; we use it as our voice. It first speaks to me and I use it to speak to others too. We attain good understanding by the Holy Spirit who helps and teaches the meaning of the holy word. The carnal mind has no capability of understanding a single word in the Bible – it misinterprets it.

The Voice and the Holy Word

Think to conceive;
Speak to receive.

The voice and the word are one and same. In the voice is also found breathe and sound which all represents authority. Here is the voice of the word or should we say the power of the word. When God said that he makes man; after forming him, we see that he breathed into his nostrils. Breathe made man a living soul. Man became active. What we have had thought and decided to see in material form and in our livelihood.

Jeremiah 1:8 *Be not afraid of their faces: for I am with thee to deliver thee, saith the LORD. 9*

Then the LORD put forth his hand, and touched my mouth. And the LORD said unto me, Behold, I have put my words in thy mouth. 10 See, I have this day set thee over the nations and over the kingdoms, to root out, and to pull down, and to destroy, and to throw down, to build, and to plant. [KJV]

The word is a tool or weapon for use to generate, form or reform and transform whatever it is that needs to be worked on. A thought is an active work of combining words to make something tangible. There is also imagination which is the making of images, measure, form and sounds of what we expect to see manifest.

Psalms 107:20 *He spoke the word that healed you, that pulled you back from the brink of death.* [MSB]

The word is alive and active. It has life in it. It activates other things to which it is sent forth to. It brings things into existence. There is a process for the things to grow. Such a one like when a seed is planted, it grows and thereafter harvest.

John 1.1 *IN THE beginning [before all time] was the Word (Christ), and the Word was with God, and the Word was God Himself.*

2. He was present originally with God.

3. All things were made and came into existence through Him; and without Him was not even one thing made that has come into being. [AMP]

Be: *existence, God ever existed.*

Beginning: *He decided to gain more good things; giving rise or original; taking rise or origin; creating and forming.*

Old English beginnan, of Germanic origin; related to Dutch and German beginnen [Oxford Dictionary]

Beginning: *The primitive Greek root means "to be long," "to draw out." It is used also to express the inauguration of a particular event* (Exo.12:2). [International Standard Bible Encyclopedia].

The voice of the word of Yahweh speaks things into existence. He makes physical materialization of things. The Lord God Yahweh brought out of the spiritual world the physical, material things we see physically. All the things were made by light. God is light. And the sons of God are light. Jesus Christ told it to the disciples that they he is the light of the word and spoke in a parable about how that no man would light a candle and put it under the table.

Colossians *1.12 giving thanks to the Father, who has qualified us to share in the inheritance of the saints in Light.* [NASB]

James 1:17 Every good gift and every perfect gift is from above, and comes down from the Father of lights, with whom there is no variation or shadow of turning. [CAB]

Daniel 2.22 *He reveals the deep and secret things; He knows what is in the darkness, and the light dwells in Him.* [LITV]

The righteous works and truth guided Daniel. David too, he consulted from Yahweh all his life. He was able to know things those magicians, sorcerers and Chaldeans failed to find out. And these were made possible because he loved to seek Yahweh's face. Whenever he faced a challenge he directed his look to the Lord his God. He made sure to leave the presence of God only when he had gotten counsel. He was appointed master over all the magicians in Babylon. He was a man who lived according to the will of God. His lifelong was about his God. He confessed and professed God's will all his life. Thus he is one of the men of valour. The right way is his power for life strength and light is his warmth.

Christ body is a seed (flesh) died, rot (while planted) in the sepulcher (garden, ground) to redeem (germinate, rebirth, regenerate, resurrect) men (sons) of eternal life.

Isaiah 9:6 For unto us a child is born, unto us a son is given: and the government shall be upon his shoulder: and his name shall be called Wonderful, Counsellor, The mighty God, The everlasting Father, The Prince of Peace. [KJV]

We were given a child who belonged to the King of kings as a gift. He was born to a chosen family as a son. He lived a sacred life to fulfill the holy works of Yahweh. The whole earthly government depends upon him; whether they know, want, wish or not. All power belongs to him in heaven and on earth. In order that the saviour might come to earth and save the lost people who fell from grace. He had to come in the form of his lost children. He grew up in the word of God. He began learning from stage one. He depended on it for his life's decisions and anointing. He learnt all the lessons needed for him to counsel his people later.

The Spirit

The Holy Spirit as we read in *Genesis 1.2 ... and the Spirit of God moved upon the face of the waters.* There was nothing made yet. We also get around a matter or we decide not to. The first time something comes before us, we begin to ask questions like - what is this? How will I get to solve it?

John 1. 4. *In Him was Life, and the Life was the Light of men.*

5. And the Light shines on in the darkness, for the darkness has never overpowered it [put it out or absorbed it or appropriated it, and is unreceptive to it]. [AMP]

If we long, we follow Christ; prolong that good song to long; to never fall low from Christ but to fall low before him.

A man who has read the word is enriched in wisdom; light is in his heart and is an enlightened man. It is an everyday keeping of the word. It is a follow through all that is said in the holy word. Prayer is made using the word. He is able to worship God in the spirit.

If knowledge is power then understanding is strength and wisdom is light.

Self-trust and trusting flesh is self-destruction.

Proverbs 3:5 *Trust GOD from the bottom of your heart; don't try to figure out everything on your own.* [MSG]

Jude 1:20 *But you, beloved, building yourselves up in your most holy faith, praying in the Holy Spirit,* [CAB]

When we are taking in water, it is because we are sure that the water is purified os better say, clean for use and has no harm. Whether that is sure or not. Fire is used to purify water and many other stuff. The tongues as of fire cannot be compared to any language that we speak on earth. The scripture is saying - 'building yourselves.' It is a master key to build up more power to use to raise the dead, heal the sick;mimed; blind and lame. It makes faith grow faster. It is a heavenly language that only Yahweh understands. the language that if one is using it, gets revitalised, rejuvenated, redeemed, restored and restituted.

Proverbs 4:23 *Above all else, guard your heart, for it affects everything you do.* [New Literal Translation]

Whatever is in the heart – stored there in is what gives man much strength to create. What we speak becomes our reality. And what we have in our hearts is what we imagine that it could be for the heart I say is the spirit. The Holy Spirit tests the faith of the spirit of man and prepares him for a holy service.

THE LIGHT

*The eyes are the lamps; the spirit is the
candle; and Holy Spirit is the light.
Physical eyes have a perfect perception
for personal perusal
And profit: In Christ it's a divine mission
oriented vision.*

"Let there be light"
The words are expressed as follows:

Let *verb - with objective and infinitive not pre-
vent or forbid; allow the infinite light to come into
existence - in/fin/ite adjective limitless or endless
in space, extent, or size; impossible to measure or
calculate;*

There - *adverb in, at, or to that place or position;*

Be - *(usu. there is/are) exist - be present - occupy*

a position in space - stay in the same place or condition - attend - come; go; visit - [as copular verb] having the state, quality, identity, nature, role, etc., specified;

Light - *mass noun the natural agent that stimulates sight and makes things visible, -count noun a source of illumination;*

You only know as much as you see.

A lamp is used to see what is around or inside the heart. It is used to see around a small radius or circumference. In simple terms near surroundings - so what do you keep seeing or looking at? That you will only know and speak of. It also stands for salvation as in Matthew 25:1. Yet a man of God needs to have light as a torch to see direction, a path, the way and destiny besides a candle. When the physical eyes which are the lamps close, man is sleeping at night. The spiritual understanding in Christ shines brighter as a greater light. Every moment a Christian gets enlightened there is light that comes to his ignorance so it disappears. A man becomes enriched, enliven and enhanced in the knowledge of the most high God.

Genesis 1:3. *And God said, Let there be light: and there was light.* [KJV]

John 1:9. *The true light, which gives light to every man, was then coming into the world.* [BBE]

Colossians 2.15 *and having despoiled principalities and powers, He made a SHOW OF THEM openly, TRIUMPHING over them in it.* [AMP]

He made a show of them or exposed what was hidden and brought it to light. He led captivity captive - he arrested those who had arrested his children. Whatever was crooked was instantly made straight. Therein regaining, restoring and restituting what he lost and his children.

For the plants to grow, they need light and warmth. And for the church to grow it needs consistent, fervent hearing of the word and prayer. The right deeds of a Christian increase the power in his authority. A Christian can only get instructions to do right from the word of Jehovah.

He broke open the strong hold, plans, bands, thought of the enemies. He is a victorious King and bears great authority and power that can never be defeated. Light is what covers all the children of Jehovah that walk in truth. It is a protection and the glory of God.

SALVATION

The word's way and God's way are whole
And the same love way in his name.

Jacob came to luz which means back bone of the spine or the body of a man then called it Bethel meaning a house of God. Luz was a place of death; a man's terrestrial (physical) body dies and it is carnal. A bone is a symbol of dryness, unfruitfulness, lack, void, hardship and uselessness. The common stone he took and put it to lay his head on, later became a rock representing Christ Jesus: headship is direction; on as a pillow for rest - after attaining salvation there is rest. In order to continue in peace someone has to keep what governs whatever is about the place. This is place of peace forever. Man might not realize that freedom from pain is already granted. And only when a man realizes then they could requested as per given liberty and provision. Life everlasting is given also.

Then, he raised it; he acknowledged, respected, adored and it became his pillar; source of strength, foundation and anchor.

Heaven is open for him to call to God. He can have heavenly supply for his all needs. The door is open for one to seek help from the most high; our judge to whom to present petitions, our voices heard and have answers. And, it is the manifestation of the glory of God. [Genesis 28.11-32] [IJohn5.14-15].

Let us break down this - Salvation and it's purpose.

John 5:1 *After this there was a feast of the Jews; and Jesus went up to Jerusalem.*

2 Now there is at Jerusalem by the sheep market a pool, which is called in the Hebrew tongue Beth-esda, having five porches.

3 In these lay a great multitude of impotent folk,

of blind, halt, withered, waiting for the moving of the water.

4 For an angel went down at a certain season into the pool, and troubled the water: whosoever then first after the troubling of the water stepped in was made whole of whatsoever disease he had. 5 And a certain man was there, which had an infirmity thirty and eight years.

6 When Jesus saw him lie, and knew that he had been now a long time in that case, he saith unto him, Wilt thou be made whole?

7 The impotent man answered him, Sir, I have no man, when the water is troubled, to put me into the pool: but while I am coming, another steppeth down before me.

8 Jesus saith unto him, Rise, take up thy bed, and walk.

9 And immediately the man was made whole, and took up his bed, and walked: and on the same day was the sabbath. [KJV]

In verse 1: After the miracle and after what comes after having read the scripture;

a feast: usually when one attains salvation, there is celebration in heaven; angels of the Lord rejoice, for the chosen people of God that have been restored back to the kingdom of Light.

In verse 2; Jesus in Jerusalem: in the vision of peace, in the city of righteousness;

by the sheep; flock, Christians' market - a place of exchange, trade area, where there is selling and buying, for example, they sell, spend their sinful lives in exchange for Jesus' life.,

a pool; water, which is the word of faith, this is the one used to buy, the one they buy, treasure, exchange of wealth on the terms of the word of God;

Bethesda, other forms occur as Bēthzathá and Bēthsaidá: it means "house of mercy."

In verse 3; it has five porches (John 10:23;

Acts 3:11; Acts 5:12). These porches are the five senses of man. I reckon that many educated people would say that they can do almost anything because their senses function well.

In here I say that there are diseases which are called incurable yet with God all things are possible;

With all the five senses functioning in man; in the spiritual realm they are unfruitful without the Holy Spirit. There lay a great multitude of impotent men who are blind. Eyes they have but they cannot see the kingdom of Jehovah; halt-Matthew 18:8, having legs which is the ability to move, yet were not able to walk and reach heaven or experience the spiritual realm fruits, it is like a dead soul: withered are men who are dead in the spirit, Mark 4:6, here the root is the spirit, it is the one that is united with Christ;

In verse 4, they waited for the moving of the water which is the preaching of the word of faith, studying, reading, until they did this, impotence would be long gone out of them.

Whosoever has faith to receive their healing

and deliverance - they are granted that healing immediately after the hearing of the word through a sermon then spoken by the mouth of a believer; this confession of redemption.

In verse 5 And a certain man was there, which had an infirmity thirty and eight years;

there was a well-known man there,

thirty eight years: there are 39 Old Testament books, now here we see that salvation was not yet come to man. Only after the thirty-ninth book, do we see, hear, learn and acknowledge the birth of the Saviour of the world, Jesus Christ: so there was always an infirmity in the lives of the people which was not washed away completely before his help.

The whole New Testament is one book. This is book number forty. He was bitten many times, forty minus one to restore his people.

While all God's people waited for I AM, a priest would step in for them to perform a service for the atonement of their sins through the sprinkling of the blood of animals. This was done for cleansing purposes. Even so, there was remembrance of sins. This means that sins were not completely forgotten.

In the tabernacle of the Lord was a priest appointed and anointed to perform services to the Lord God for the people. Sacrifices for burnt, sin and peace offering were made once every year. And all the people came to sacrifice at the acceptable time of the Lord.

In verse 6; When Jesus saw him lie, and knew that he had been now a long time in that case, he saith unto him, Wilt thou be made whole?

The man was helpless, confused and had no hope for the future because in 38 years past he hardly had seen himself to getting a chance of getting healed completely.

Therefore the son of man came to him and asked if he was willing to see a miracle. God almighty made man in his image and gave him authority and dominion on earth. So he asked permission to perform a miracle from man.

In verse 7; the man answered that he had no man to help him; in this very manner the people of God in the Old testament would answer that their infirmity had no way to be wholly purged away.

The lame man trusted in the arm of the flesh. The only way they could work was to sacrifice for the sins, though the conscience was not cleansed to forget about old sins.

So the man explained that when a time to be healed came, his neighbour would step in before him.

There was a priest assigned to step into the holy of holies to sacrifice for all the people's sins year after year;

In verse 8; Jesus came and spoke a word and said, rise; look to God through his word, take up your bed: his rest in Christ; and move from his burdens, pain, disease and carry his cross; walk: follow Christ, walk in him.

In verse 9; The man took his bed; he actually left the place of torment and slavery to sin. He stood up and started walking freely. After Sabbath men entered eternal rest; they confess with their mouths and believe in their hearts that Jesus is Lord and attain unto salvation.

After creation – God rested;
After salvation – man rested.

CHRIST THE BREAD

Bread

The bread, lump and dough are made by flour from wheat are acceptable for use in the house of God. All things were made by the word including food. Man does not live by bread alone but by every word which comes out of the mouth of God. God told Elijah to arise and eat to have strength for the journey was great.

Ephesians 1:6 *to the praise of the glory of His grace, by which He bestowed favor upon us in the Beloved.* [CAB]

We also find that in John 3.16. He further said to the disciples to be aware of the leaven of the Pharisees. The yeast or leaven talked about is sin. A little sin makes one fail to enter heaven.

Small things that men do, say and workout are what lets man attain rewards in heaven. While on earth, men should recognize that no small act will go unnoticed when it comes to being considered worthy to be called sons of God and worth of his glory.

Galatians 5.9 *And please don't toss this off as insignificant. It only takes a minute amount of yeast, you know, to permeate an entire loaf of bread.* [MSG]

A little sin is all that makes man a sinner. The Bible says that no ungodliness shall enter the kingdom of God.

I Corinthians 5.6 *Your glorying is not good. Know ye not that a little leaven leaveneth the whole lump?*

7. Purge out therefore the old leave that ye may be a new lump, as ye are unleavened (holy). For even the Messiah our Passover (Exodus 12.11) is sacrificed for us:

8. Therefore let us keep the feast, not with old leaven (sin), neither with the leaven of malice and wickedness; but with the unleavened bread of sincerity and truth. [KJV]

The lump represents life and unleavened represents a holy livelihood; and leaven representing sin. The Levites were instructed by Moses and him by God almighty to offer animal blood of

Bullocks, rams and lambs to sprinkle for the forgiveness of sins. Therefore we see the teachings of the law and get to the new covenant of the blood of the Lamb of God's teachings concerning the better things that Christ accomplishes for us.

Hebrews 8:5 *These serve as a copy and shadow of the heavenly things, as Moses was warned when he was about to complete the tabernacle. For He said, Be careful that you make everything according to the pattern that was shown to you on the mountain.* [HCSB]

The old testament is the reflection of the New Testament. The shadow of better things is the promise found in the old testament that the Saviour was going to come and save all his people. One sacrifice settled all debts that his poeple had to the slavery of sin. He is love.

Love deferred is life deterred.

The love or the fear of the Lord draws man to the Lord God. It is love that keeps man in genuine worship and honour. If a man has love then they can know what it is that are doing and it is the reason to live uprightly.
[Proverbs 8.17]

Hebrews 10:1 *1 FOR SINCE the Law has merely a rude outline (foreshadowing) of the good things to come--instead of fully expressing those things--it can never by offering the same sacrifices continually year after year make perfect those who approach [its altars].* [AMP]

When Jesus becomes a personal Saviour of a

man. They are able to discern between right and wrong. In the new Testament, we see that Paul emphesizes that when we look into the holy word, we start to become what we look at; the image of Jesus Christ.

The law, shadow and image

The shadow

A shadow is a *noun a dark area or shape produced by a body coming between rays of light and a surface.* [Oxford Dictionary].

The Old Testament is the shadow of Salvation that we see in Acts chapter 2. It (shadow) is something that has nothing much to be talked about. It does have much significance as it follows man and appears whenever necessary. Just as a signature does look similar to the name of one who has signed. It only shows significance when a person is intending to agree to a commitment. This is in day light when all men are awake. When there is light that puts all things openly as those in agreement and witnesses can agree.

An Image – *noun a representation or similitude of any person or thing formed of a material substance; as an image wrought out of stone, wood or wax. The representation of any person or thing: an object of worship. The second commandment forbids the worship of images; the likeness of anything on canvas; a picture; a resemblance painted; any copy, representation or likeness.*

Whose is this image and superscription? Matthew 22: Superscription - *designating the person in whose honour or by whose authority it is issued.*

However an inscription is testimony of authority. It has the very significance as that of word of mouth from a person who holds authority. The image inscription of a man with authority is true worth of his influence.

The inscription holds the authority behind it. It is so even after the death of the one who once signed it on the paper and any other place where it is imprinted on. Men that follow and keep the law behind the law are aware of what they stand for.

There is no legal document that does not require to be signed for validation. Our properties has title deeds that show ownership rights. Otherwise, anyone can claim ownership of whatever lacks owner's rights.

I have seen a man occupy a building for a long time. When time comes to see were the owner is and no else comes forward to claim; the very person who is present attains legal ownership. Finally, we should

own our knowledge; professing what we believe in.

THE LAW

The law is written as a shadow of things to come. People see the shadow. The question is how is it formed? When light hits an opaque - something that does not allow light to pass through it, a shadow is evident.

Jesus is that <u>object</u> of the casted shadow or the subject. Letters as subjects of Jesus are written with dead ink – like a shadow on a piece of paper.

The object is the force and the subject is cause of the force behind it. The light casts the shadow of the object. Anyone can buy the Bible with money but to buy the truth in it; we use faith and the love of God almighty. We should accept Christ Jesus and his works towards, within and for us. We should accept his works and the worker of the evident works.

We can look at dreams and visions the same way. They are very real to the man who is having them. They are mostly and vividly imprinted in the mind and the heart.

The shadow and Image

The word: food of the spiritual man, a Christian; reason that the LAW was given to men. It was written on a stone by the hand of God and given to Moses his servant. God then promised to write the LAW on the hearts of men meaning those who have had received Christ Jesus as their personal Saviour.

The reflection of man in the mirror is the real image of the man standing before the mirror. The image signifies the Rhema word; the spiritual word. The image is also the vision.

Romans 2:15 *Which shew the work of the law written in their hearts, their conscience also bearing witness, and their thoughts the mean*

while accusing or else excusing one another;)

The conscience helps us stand firm in Christianity. They are able to discern between right and wrong. To fear God is to love God which is the first commandment of the Law [Ephesians 2.15]. The letter kills but the Spirit gives life.

The written letter for to the later and latter time.
Even the law is the shadow.

The Law is a shadow of better things and a new covenant of everlasting life. It was accomplished on resurrection day of Jesus Christ. One sacrifice made once for all. A shadow can be said to be an example. It is not a complete real thing but a sign that there is something more real to which it is attached. A shadow is a copy but stands for the real man and an object. The written word, law or logos was given to man as it was the shadow of an everlasting covenant of promise to come to be made manifest by the blood of Jesus. Christ is love.

Love is a root; Man is a plant.
Let Christ feed the need of the root,
And get the right fruits.

Love is a root. If Christ is the vine; we are the branches and the father is the husbandman. We are to be rooted and grounded by love in him to produce good spiritual fruits. The function of roots to a tree is that they obtain air, mineral elements and water for the plants or trees. If the roots were consuming acidic water it definitely would suffocate the plant which eventually dies later. This stands to reveal that it collects substances of things to their place. It connects two sides. It acquires what is needed by the recipient. It pulls wants and needs close to man and to God. It makes the tree stand firm in the particular place. It builds and supports the tree structure. It keeps the genealogy of the tree. If a tree's branches were to be cut off, it could still bud and begin to grow again.

Christians who keep in remembrance there source of help and power excel in all they do. The purpose of all promising journeys is in the root and reason for all that is involved and needed to proceed. The love of the holy word is power. The power for use in everthing concerning life on earth.

Every Christian's journey has a divine destiny and destination. The steps are definite in accordance with the Lord's command and will. These works are written in the holy word.

The vision of the journey gets its course intact for its core perfection and command line duty. A journey is supposed to be taken with a willing intent and focus. The talk and walk are all concerned with the value of the journey.

Man bends an ear to hear the call and instructions of the Lord according to his word and in his word.

I have a Christ Jesus journey I neither

jiggle nor joggle not.

PROMISE

A promise *noun is a declaration or assurance that one will do something or that a particular thing will happen.* [Oxford dictionary]

[with objective] pledge [with objective.] give good grounds for expecting (a particular occurrence).

It was given to Abraham by our God almighty. He told him that he was going to bless him with children's children as the sand on the seashore.

In Genesis 22.16 *I have sworn by Myself, says the* **Lord,** *because you have done this thing, and on* **My account have not spared your beloved son,**

17. *surely blessing I will bless you, and multi-plying I will multiply your seed as the stars of heaven, and as the sand which is by the shore of the sea, and your seed shall inherit the cities of their enemies.*

18. *And in your seed shall all the nations of the earth be blessed, because you have obeyed My voice.* [KJV]

Hebrews 12.24 *and to Jesus, the mediator of a new covenant, and to the sprinkled blood, which speaks better than the blood of Abel.* [NASB]

Hebrews says that we put Jesus, the word as the one to decide what's best for us. We need to buy meaning that we accept the bread that gives life eternal without money. The money is represented by believing and faith. The blood of Jesus who had no sin was given to pay for the corrupt seed of Adam's sinful blood. The person who had lost hope finally got all they needed to face Yahweh through Jesus.

Buy [with objective] 1) *obtain in exchange for payment.* 2) [Informal] *accept the truth of.* [Oxford Dictionary]

So if there is payment to be made, it has been paid already by the blood of the Lamb of God. As in this scripture –

Isaiah 55.1 *"Ho, every one that thirsteth, come ye to the waters; and he that hath no money, come ye, buy, and eat; yea, come, buy wine and milk without money and without price.*

2. Why do ye spend money for that which is not bread, and your labor for that which satisfieth not? Hearken diligently unto Me, and eat ye that which is good, and let your soul delight itself in fatness. [KJV]

James 1:17 *Every good gift and every perfect gift is from above, coming down from the Father of lights with whom there is no variation or shadow due to change.* [ESV]

To buy milk which is righteousness and honey which is the holiness or glory is to agree to receive Jesus as a personal saviour. Men are free to get from Yahweh gifts of life for free at which the promise is thereby fulfilled. Jesus warned the disciples against leavened bread. He said a little yeast leavens the whole lump. The bread came - grace came to the world. They search out a word that suits their egos. Their desire is to profit selfishly from the word which they read. If it warns them against their intents of doing wrong they begin to avoid it even when it convicts them. Sometimes they want a chapter and verse where their name should be written or indicated their sin and application to their specific selfish need and plan.

In doing so, they cannot use faith; they profit nothing from the holy word. If they attend church, they remain the same; no growth evident in their particular lives. In other words, they cannot believe, accept the truth. In such lives is no righteous deed.

The holy word is a gift for all who require peace. Also reading the word without faith is as good as nothing. The baptism of the spirit helps man understand the purpose of the holy word. It is what makes the word become alive in life. The word cannot be separated from Jesus Christ and if so we lose both the power and the meaning.

John 5:39 *Search the Scriptures; for in them ye think ye have eternal life: and they are they which testify of me.*

BREAD OF LIFE

Unleavened Bread contains the most vital ingredients that we know materially, they are five things and 5 is a number that signifies grace and also seen to tell Christians about the five-fold ministry. The process that takes it to be made ready for use in homes is well known too. Jesus is the Bread of life.

Spiritually, we find that the same substances have a deep significance from the word of the Lord God. Thus we are set prepared for his holy will. We pray to request from ; access what is in heaven. Everything is further interpreted in this manner.

Life	wheat; dough; flour	breath
Light	fire	glory
Word	water	voice
Truth	salt	righteousness; purity
Spirit	oil	wine; holiness

The breath has Oxygen which supports life as we may know scientifically. Oxygen is the most expensive food in man's life. Yet it has been given freely to man by Jehovah. It is also called the breath of life: God's power of life. This life is in man and begins to plan to make bread. He speaks of what he has thought about. The breathe produces life to the dry bones that could be found in any situations.

1 Kings 17.12: the Widow had a handful of meal, oil in a cruse. She went on to say that she was to gather two sticks and prepare the meal for herself and her son that they would eat and die. But, Elijah had brought hope to her house.

The two sticks talked about here are explained in the book of Ezekiel 37.15: One stick is for

Judah and his companions the children of Israel and the other stick is the for Joseph, Ephraim and for all the house of Israel his companions. At this moment in time, the people of the kingdom of Israel were divided.

And the Lord had spoken through Ezekiel that he would bring them together again, according to his holy word in - Ezekiel 37.17. The same way we see that when the cross where Jesus was hunged; two sticks were put together. He said "it is finished" to mean that the scripture had been fulfilled.

The Bible says that wine is best kept in new wine skin. Wine is the old word used for a meer juice or sweetened edible drink without alcohol in it. The holy word is to be kept in a repentant heart. The wine is the Holy Spirit. A sinful heart would not have place for the holy word. It is going to be obvious that hearing the word preached would make such a person uncomfortable. When the Holy Spirit comes in a man; it makes his heart joyful.

Jesus told the Pharisees that he was the bread of life. If anyone ate his body; they would hunger no more. If anyone drunk his blood; they would thirst no more. He also told the woman at the water well that he gave water that that if man drunk it, it removes thirsty eternally. The number of them all was 70 disciples; but after hearingthat they should eat his body - the word and drink his blood - the word. He only remained with 12 disciples. The reason is that they lacked understanding. He had a hard speech; it required that they become spiritually learned to be able to know his language.

The word is the voice that works miracles, signs and wonders in purity. The word is the voice that gets the lost back to their father who is in heaven. The word in the bread of life is the drink that when men take it in and would never thirst again.

The five things we are to look at have to work together to make something of a lifelong importance - water, salt, oil, flour and fire.

1. WATER

It is used for diverse purposes. In bread making it collects, connects and or binds the ingredients together. In the word of God it has a core value of cleansing, the pasture of his flock and is the very word of God. It becomes a Christian voice that is used to answer all life's questions or challenges. The process of growth in Christianity needs application of the word daily. As it is written in -

John 15.3 *You are already clean because of the word which I have spoken to you.* [KJV]

Some have said to me that they usually felt better after attending church services. The grace of his presence is in his commuinion. It purifies our minds. It gets rid of the bad memories, hardships that mind make on their own and quickens the spirit of man. For the mind to come to the upright standard of God; it is through the word.

A service is [verb [with obj.] perform routine maintenance or repair work on (a vehicle or machine). In a general sense a labour of body or of body and mind, performed at the command of a superior, or the pursuance of duty, or for the benefit of another. Service is voluntary or involuntary - [Webster Bible Dictionary].

According to the word of God, a service is the repairing of the Spirit of man. This is giving what they have to get renewed to a better state. A man gives God his soul, mind and strength to get better and regenerated. Growth and profit comes through service to God.

The word works all things in man's life. The word is the sword of the spirit. It is a weapon necessary for use in times of warfare; spoken to produce the said results. And it is also a staff for a Christian man's welfare; it is engage for warfare and used for various use as aid.

Ephesians 5:26 *that He might sanctify it, cleansing it by the washing of the water in the Word,* [LITV]

Proverbs 18:4 *The words of a man's mouth are deep waters; the fountain of wisdom is a bubbling brook.* [ESV]

With the word inside his heart, he speaks his belief and witnesses the manifestation thereof. The word spoken in holiness creates good things men benefit from and brings peace.

The fellowship with the Lord Yahweh is best done when the holy word is filled in the heart. The best way to speak to him is in the word. The way to follow to find him is in the word. The whole system of the kingdom of light is in the word. He also requires from us to ask for understanding.

2. SALT

It is a preservative. The value and importance of seasoned food is certain after applying salt to it. This stands to give meaning for a good purpose. Adds meaning to the taste of food. Flies would not come where there is salt - demons can't find place to be near a man who is well seasoned in with the holy word. It bonds the value of the food and the desire of a man to get satisfaction from it; men who meet a man with good salt to say that such men have good counsel, benefit from such. It builds the desire to have the same thing used for so many times - people will come again and again to get upright counsel. It defines and emphasizes the very kind of thing and what is been taken in the mouth. By it, a Christian preserves the relationship with his Father in heaven.

Now, pertaining to Lot's wife turning into a pillar of salt; it is simply to say that she became a sign to apply to our personal lives; in every day's life as an example for those who may wish to decide to turn away from following Jesus Christ and keeping his charge. It is the truth of his life's worth and treasure.

Leviticus 2.13 *And every oblation of thy meat offering shalt thou season with salt; neither shalt thou suffer the salt of the covenant of thy Elohim to be lacking from thy meat offering: with all thine offerings thou shalt offer salt.*

14. *And if thou offer a meat offering of thy first-fruits unto YHWH, thou shalt offer for the meat offering of thy first-fruits green ears of corn dried by the fire, even corn beaten out of full ears.* [KJV]

Ezra 6.9 *And whatever is needed--bulls, rams, or sheep for burnt offerings to the God of heaven, wheat, salt, wine, or oil, as the priests at Jerusalem require--let that be given to them day by day without fail,*

10. *that they may offer pleasing sacrifices to the God of heaven and pray for the life of the king and his sons.*

11. *Also I make a decree that if anyone alters this edict, a beam shall be pulled out of his house, and he shall be impaled on it, and his house shall be made a dunghill.* [ESV]

Matthew 5:13 *"You are salt for the Land. But if salt becomes tasteless, how can it be made salty again? It is no longer good for anything except being thrown out for people to trample on.* [CJB]

Savor - *The primary meaning of the word is "taste," "flavour" (from Latin sapor, "taste"). But generally it has the meaning of "smell," "odour": It gives value, importance to the food.* [Webster 1828 dictionary]

Whatever action and work of such a seasoned man in the holy word has flavour. Salt in Christianity represents righteousness. It is being right with God almighty and doing right. Something worth of salt is something that teaches good morals. Salt is needed and helpful in many different ways. Salt preserves and protects food - same as righteousness protects Christians. It extends the lifespan of food on the shelf - a Christian life is prolonged and preserved too. The word of Yahweh has power to make us be well kept in all seasons. It is however a necessity for long life. In Isaiah chapter 61, the oil of gladness is talked about. It says that when there oil; the anointing, men would rejoice. It is easy to praise God.

Mark 9:49 *For every man will be salted with fire, and every sacrifice will be salted with salt material.*

50 The salt material is good, but if the salt material becomes saltless, by what will ye season it? Have salt in yourselves, and be at peace among each other. [ACV]

Everyone shall become righteous after passing through a test of their faith by fire; Sacrificing is righteousness.

In verse 50 Righteousness is good: but if a righteous man lose their authority and right, they would not live up to please God, who endues them with power. The authority is used to judge - command a disease to depart from the body it is affecting with immediate effect. It is used to teach simply; making others understand the holy word.

They want rest; they wrestle
They want a testimony; they are in a test of faith.

Revelation 3:18 I advise you to buy from Me gold having been fired by fire, that you may be rich; and white garments, that you may be clothed, and your shame and nakedness may not be revealed. And anoint your eyes with eye salve, that you may see. [LITV]

Salve - *A glutinous composition or substance to be applied to wounds or sores; when spread on leather or cloth, it is called a plaster.*
- To help or remedy by a salvo, excuse or reservation. [Webster 1828 Dictionary]

We may see everything around but need not follow everything about. We should to repair our sight so that we have our focus fixed to Christ's teaching, instructions, work and knowledge. Christ has given all we need to have to step well in the valley of the shadow of death. One man with good eyes is able to lead people to better places. The church is urged to have spiritual eyes that can magnify the word of God and see his salvation always. The scripture says we have to have one eye. The body of Christ depends on the eyes that they may see Christ in everything they are doing to the glory of God. One eye that Jesus emphasised on is focus and steadfstness.

This is teaching us to have one master. The only purpose to serve. The only reason to hold on to.

Looking at one thing; the Bible - we are assured that the results are getting us greater good.

3. OIL

It is the anointing of God endowed on his people. The Bible says the unity or the coming together of brethren together is like oil poured on the head of Aaron running down to his beards and to his garments. This is the blessing of unction by the Lord God. In the book of 1 Kings 17.12 Prophet Elijah visited the widow. He told her to prepare for him Bread. She answered that only had a little meal, oil as the main commodities.

Crude Oil is the source of energy for vehicles, planes and machinery fuel. It is also used to make polythene materials for clothes. It is also the source of lubricants that reduce or remove friction and rust. To the wheels of a cart, they apply it to reduce friction. Like the covering of the children of God is the light or fire. This is also called the anointing. Lust is the infirmities and iniquities in the soul of a man. The lust of the eyes and that of the world can corrupt man's soul. the thing that can negatively affect and destroy a pure life.

The blessing on a man's life will touch many other lives for great development. It is the one that allows fire to burn inside of the flour of the dough and or lump. Also it is smeared on the tray to avoid dough from sticking to the tray after baking the bread. Oil is applied in lamps for light.

When the Holy Spirit enters man, he becomes regenerated. He is transfigured. Jesus said what comes out of a man corrupts him. Oil signifies holy baptism, it is the holy sanctification. An offering was made unto God.

Leviticus 2.15 *Put olive oil on it, and lay frankincense on it; it is a grain offering.* [Complete Jewish Bible]

God almighty anointed David as king by sending Samuel to the house of Jesse. He was the youngest in his family yet chosen for a high position. The moment after anointing he went on to kill a bear, Lion, when danger came against the sheep he was looking after, the Spirit of might came upon him. He slew the beasts. Later, the giant Goliath from the Philistines' army came against the army of the Israelites; David used a stone from his sling. David knew that he was well armoured and ready for war in the name of the Lord. This knowledge that the Almighty is the greastest of all, is weaponry. It is one used to keep steady and stable and to avoid staggering.

Matthew 25:4 *The wise, however, took oil in jars along with their lamps.* [NIV]

Oil represents salvation, and saying this is personal. When one is saved, he cannot use personal salvation to represent the whole nation. Every man has a get their own salvation to enter heaven. It is used to kindle fire. This fire can be for burning, cooking or lighting up a place. In Psalms chapter 133 it represents anointing for impartation to do the service of

Yahweh. It enables men to do what they cannot do without it. A man with the oil is able to pray for the other man without the oil to receive from Yahweh. A sick man will get healed by this oil. The oil is used to sanctify staffs – clothes, water to administer to the need. The people with sickness are in dire need. The oil signifies the Holy Ghost. The Holy Ghost purifies the sons of God seven times as Gold is purified so. This seven times means completely and thoroughly purifying.

4. FLOUR

It is food for the body, soul and Word of God is food for the Holy Spirit. Just like Oxygen - it sustains life. It is required to be taken daily - the holy word has the equal function in a particular Christian life. It is supposed to be chewd enough before swallowing its.

Flour: *a powder obtained by grinding grain, typically wheat, and used to make bread, cakes, and pastry.* [Oxford dictionary]

The dough, lump, animal or the food has to be unleavened. It has to be acquired by our own strength and in legitimate ways. Man has to stand before the King of kings without blemish [Ezra 6.9]. This is the food that was usually in Israel given for sacrifices in the temple. This is what Christians are to be doing to live holy unto God.

It is required of a Christian to bring to food to the house of God that there may be food in his house. His ministers; the Levites offered sacrifices and stood in the presence of God to pray for his people. For the service to God, they did eat of what the people gave and continued to minister there in the house of God. People took meat offerings for the priest which God command Moses the Israelites to do. This is done to bring everlasting provision in their lives because they give as unto God. He requires that his children do as stated in his precepts of his word.

Numbers 15.18 *'Speak to the Israelites and say: "When you have entered the country to which I am bringing you,*

19. *you will set a portion aside for Yahweh when you eat that country's bread.*

20. *You will set one cake aside as the first-fruits of your dough; you will set this offering aside like the one set aside from your threshing.*

21. *For all future generations you will set a portion of your dough aside for Yahweh.* [New Jerusalem Bible]

In the King James version the word here is used - Heave [hiːv] **1.** verb *(past and past participle heaved hove)* 1) *[with obj. and adverbial of direction] lift or haul (something heavy) with great effort 2) [with objective. To produce]* [Oxford Dictionary]

People of God have to lift, give the best offering to worship God with their substance. Worshipping God with substance is giving God the best there is in one's life. If one has money, it has to worship God through offering. Worship is an act towards God. If someone does business and gets money from someone in dishonesty and adds to his own as his own, it makes all he has not worthy of honesty. It affects all he owns. Where the treasure is, there the heart is. We give more attention to a place where we get profit.

Nehemiah 10.37 *Moreover, we will bring to the storerooms of the house of our God, to the priests, the first of our ground meal, of our grain offerings, of the fruit of all our trees and of our new wine and oil. And we will bring a tithe of our crops to the Levites, for it is the Levites who collect the tithes in all the towns where we work.* [NIV]

The custom of earthly kings is that when they visit one another. They carry gifts from their land to give to the fellow king they are paying a visit. This is the best produce that their kingdom has in offer. Also they come back with best gifts from where they would have gone to visit. They would carry riches of Gold, Silver, pomegranate, frankincense as we can see in scriptures. The three wise men who visited Jesus Christ after his birth in the kraal had the best offering for a new born king. It is written to say, do not go to a King without an offering in your hands.

It is an ancient custom for kings to bring gifts

when visiting one another's kingdoms. Queen Basheba visited King Solomon and brought with her much Gold. We give praise, honour, power and glory due to the king of kings.

5. FIRE

In the book of Revelation, chapter 2, Jesus requires that a man be warm and not lukewarm. He states that men should not be cold nor lukewarm. If they are lukewarm he would spew them out. Daily services that Christians do towards the Lord God make them hot with the holy fire of the Holy Ghost. It is the power of God. It is used to warm ourselves. It is what burns evil things that trouble his children, melts their darts, arrows, poison and spears of destruction.

The fire prepares the saints for service; a tool for sanctification, absolute washing from sin; deliverance, from evil; purging sin, take infirmities or iniquities from man's soul and a covering, protection from enemies and possible destruction and corruption. The greatest armory in the history of war; worn to protect the body in battle.

Christians are the light of this world; a lamp cannot be put under the table. It is power to bring newness to many things that pass through it for purification. This fire scotches the chaff and that which remains is what is required for dedicated service to God. When the 3 Hebrew boys were put in the blast furnace, those who pushed them inside caught the fire and were burnt to death. As Gold is tested seven times, the word was tested by fire. Jesus Christ was sent to seven witnesses before being taken away to be crucified.

Intense heat that comes from electric power is what produces light. Where there greater light there is a revelation; it guides our destination and destiny. Light within the spirit reveals what is inside the heart and mind. It helps and makes Christians know what they really want to certainly act on. This is full knowledge; it brings us to understanding and revelation of matters. Then light around us exposes what we have around us. Light before our eyes is for direction.

Jesus Christ yoke is easy and his burden is light. A yoke is the union of Jesus and man; working together on earth for a greater good. It is a partnership of two interest parties in a holy covenant. He says that man be carrying his own cross and follow him in the kingdom of light.

"His burden is light" – his work has knowledge, instructions and tools fully provided for. These are found in the word of God. A man learns righteousness from Jesus and attains unto light. His life power gives light. All things are right in him so following through them thoroughly is begetting revelation of life eternal. Spiritual provision brings easiness to every work before us. Work is done as it flows without lack of power or necessities to use.

Intense light has been used to kill cancer cells which is called chemotherapy.

Light *noun* *[mass noun] the natural agent that stimulates sight and makes things visible; [count noun] a source of illumination* [Oxford Dictionary]

Matthew 5.14. *"You are the light of the world. A city set on a hill cannot be hidden. 15. Nor do people light a lamp and put it under a basket, but on a stand, and it gives light to all in the house. 16. In the same way, let your light shine before others, so that they may see your good works and give glory to your Father who is in heaven.* [ESV]

Psalms 119:105 *Your word is a lamp that gives light wherever I walk.* [CEV]

In a lamp oil is added that it produces fire. We use a lamp to search well where we stand or where we are supposed to step as well as light to get a clear vision of what is in front while on the journey. This is also the work of the word of God that helps us see our surrounding and beyond. The word is used to search which better steps or decisions to take. It is used to check our surroundings; including where to sit and where to place our lives.

Acts 2:3 *And there appeared to them dividing tongues, as of fire, and they settled upon each one of them.* [A Conservative Version]

The disciples began to speak a heavenly holy language that only Jehovah can understand. The spirit of man utters things that man cannot understand. Earthly soldiers have a language that their enemies barely understand. Fire is distinct but its composition can never be understood but only be seen and felt. Its affect and effect is evident through everyday livelihood. Fire was used to create all things in heaven and earth and it will be used to remove all these things in order to usher in the new things.

1Corinthians 3:13 *each man's* work *will become manifest; for the Day will disclose it, because it will be revealed with fire, and the fire will test what sort of work each one has done.* [Revised Standard Version]

God reveals the intentions of man by fire; his holiness and glory. In this is man set well with God. The bible calls the son of God as children of the day in the book of 1 Thessalonians chapter 5.

Hebrews 12.29 *for also, "Our God is a consuming fire."* Deut. 4:24 [LITV]

The process of the written word is to bear fruit of holiness into the physical world and is unbreakable. The written word; the law has terms, conditions and promises in its statutes. The conditions need to be followed according to ordinances therein, Joshua 1.8. These promises are evident when man reads, watches over, hears, meditates upon, keeps; lets the mind stay on the word and these are truth, light, holiness, purity and life everlasting in his heart and is reminded of it always. They are sure.

Philippians 4.8 *Finally, brethren, whatsoever things are true, whatsoever things are honest,* *whatsoever things are just, whatsoever things are pure, whatsoever things are lovely, whatsoever things are of good report; if there be any virtue, and if there be any praise, think on these things.* [KJV]

Only Christ Jesus of Nazareth is true, honest, just, pure, has virtue and is worthy of praise always. "Let everything that has breathe praise the Lord". We got to think on such things and especially on God the father and Jesus Christ that are worthy of praise - we begin to praise in order to get virtue. If one begins to praise wrong things he is later affected by them. A good report from heaven was brought through Joseph and Mary the mother of Jesus in the lineage of King David. She kept them in her heart and pondered deeply on them. The next verse says that those who search to know whether the things in scriptures be of good report and results thereafter. Surely, these people who do such are noble. They were more highly respected in that generation.

Acts 17:11 *These were more noble than those in*

Thessalonica, in that they received the word with all readiness of mind, and searched the scriptures daily, whether those things were so. [1833 Webster Bible]

Children of God like Daniel and the other three Hebrew boys who gave their time to studying the word of Yahweh their Father in holy faith; got matured and could be able to resist evil. They understood Yahweh's law and were able to stand firm before kings.

Daniel 1:4 *young men in whom was no blemish, but who were of good appearance and having understanding in all wisdom, having knowledge and understanding learning, even those with strength in them to stand in the king's palace, and to teach them the writing and the language of the Chaldeans.* [LITV]

The word will help a man to endure on earth. The word has to be read, heard and heard in order to walk in the word of faith and life. The spirit requires and needs the word just as the body needs food. When one understands well, he could be well led. First, the word enters through ears to the mind, brain. The brain says I do not decide alone, then the message is sent to the heart; herein our final decision is always taken, thus the mouth speaks. Believing is living for the right that we stand for.

Romans 10.10 *For with the heart man believeth unto righteousness...* [KJV]

Romans 10:17 *Consequently, faith comes from hearing the message, and the message is heard through the word of Christ.* [NIV]

When using a phone, immediately we call someone we say, hello, waiting to hearing from the other side. If they respond hello, then we are connected. That is how we learn faith. When a young boy is told something and repeats the instruction, by repeating it; he would do exactly step by step showing that he has understood. Language is learnt in the same manner. It is instruction per instruction and action after action according to instruction given. It is voice pause, pose and response in voice or action. The Father and the Son who are respectively the Authority and the power come into oath. Wherefore man hears, listens to the word enough to see, follow and allow it rule in his heart and around his life and world.

Psalms 119.11 *I have laid thy word up in my heart that I might not sin against thee.* [ACV]

The more the instructions are clearly understood the better the steps to keep and follow them. To be informed is to have a vision and a strong hold that fortifies the city. A city is kept alive by the vision of its future and is thereby strengthened.

The more the understanding; energy is increased after this knowledge; power. So someone gets enough understanding to have revelation; light. The light is the force to use to create.

2 Peter 2:8 *for that upright man, living among them, was outraged in his upright soul by the crimes that he saw and heard every day.* [New Jerusalem Bible]

Lot lived in a sinful city called Sodom where it is likely difficult for good morals to be kept. It has become so vivid that along our modern roadsides are billboards to remind the people about the products or services different companies offer to the society; making them see that information whenever they use that particular route. It is the marketing of the companies in business and it repays them high sales.

The bible says that bad company corrupts good morals. Yet, Lot kept the faith of the Lord by keeping the word before his eyes always. And he hid it in his heart. In the new testament, the Bible says that his soul was vexed daily. Though, he was troubled thus far, Jesus was there for and with him.

Jesus is the bright morning star. He is the bright - the noon and the day; the faithful, upright one.

He is the morning - the twilight, source of light and the sunrise; he sustains lives.

And finally he is the star - the sunset and the evening; time to prepare and one who prepares us for better things.

FULFILLED PROMISE

*A promise to a man is a promise to all generations;
and a promise to everyone is a promise to none.*

Jesus was given as a child of promise to God's people. Mary received a message of promise that she would bear a son. The son would bring salvation to the Israelites. Abraham's children who are the Israelites are entitled to the promises of Jehovah towards Abraham. The scripture says that not all that are born in Israel are Israelites. God chose to give eternal life to those that would willingly turn from their wicked ways, humble themselves; pass through consecration and pray; seek the face of the holy one. The promises are fulfilled when the written word is spoken by faith through the lips. The manifestation then takes place in order to be witnessed physically and that men may believe. Man confesses with his own lips of the things God has promised him. Romans 10.10 *...and with the mouth confession is made unto **salvation**.* It was written by God, read by Abraham then meditated upon. It was told to Abraham that it was to come to his descendants: building holy Faith, the love of God almighty and edifying the body of Christ, to fit all that has been predestined by the Lord God Jehovah even to us-ward. As David hoped in the promises of God:

Psalms 119:81 *(Kaf) My soul languishes for thy salvation; I hope in thy word.* [Revised Standard Version]

In Proverbs 8.17 it shows us that the relationship benefits of holiness are surely mutual love for love. What you give is what you get. When one gives, the act and what they gave becomes a sacred blessing. In this a promise is fulfilled.

Philemon 1:5 *Hearing of thy love, and of the faith which thou hast towards the Lord Jesus and* *towards all the saints,* [Rotherham Emphasized Bible]

You can only fulfill what you absolutely know well about. It is work for a man to live in salvation. A man who loves to hear from God is assured of abundance therein fulfilling the holy work of righteousness. Hearing from Yahweh is reading his word.

I read in **Ephesians 2:19** *So then you are no longer strangers and foreigners, but you are fellow citizens with the saints, and of the household of God,* [World English Bible]

Colossians 2.19 *and not holding the head, from which all the body--through the joints and bands gathering supply, and being knit together--may increase with the increase of God.* [Young Literal Translation]

We could be in congregations or in a bible study group, only if we are rooted in Christ then nourishment is granted for increase. The fruits of the Spirit are evident in our lives for all to be admonished with. Finally we see in these scriptures that follow, they show how wonderful it is to know the Lord Jesus and accept him as lord and Saviour. We become liberated from bondage to a glorious living.

I Corinthians 15.49 *And as we have borne a resemblance to the earthy one, let us see to it that we also bear a resemblance to the heavenly One.* [1912 Weymouth New Testament]

The eyes see; ears hear and the heart keeps the promise. The heart controls the work of keeping it. The image or shadow or word we look at when reading the bible is Christ Jesus himself. The likeness, works and stature are all like Jesus. What somebody puts before their eyes often later becomes part of their lives. First it is set in the mind, in the heart then he acts on it. This act becomes character after many days of consistent commitment. The character manifest means that we're grafted in Christ the vine and rooted as branches. When the branches grow longer; they can feed fruits that they produce to other people.

When we are mindful enough on something - we gradually get fully informed on it. We get informed and programmed (kept in mind) by eye or ear contact to that information wherefore we are programmed all about it. That information dominates our conscious and then the subconscious mind - conscience. It is the mind of the heart that makes character. It makes us do what we naturally know.

It might seem as if there are external forces controlling a person whose character is developed.

What you believe, there you belong and become.

II Corinthians 3.17 *Now, "ADONAI" in this text means the Spirit. And where the Spirit of*

ADONAI is, there is freedom.

18. So all of us, with faces unveiled, see as in a mirror the glory of the Lord; and we are being changed into his very image, from one degree of glory to the next, by ADONAI the Spirit. [CJB]

If we believe what the word says, that written word – Bible. If meditated upon in our minds, understood and used practically; lived on, thereon are exercising the things of the spirit. We look as in a mirror; we get transformed in our image and become as Christ. As young babes we are to desire the sincere milk of the word to grow thereby.

It is more than a promise when a Christian is looking into the word of God. The message and the manifestation are all in one. The message is the instruction and unction - so it has manifest work. The holy word is Jesus Christ who is the messenger and the message of the fulfilled promise.

A heart with short hands cannot touch

the hem of Christ Jesus garment.